EXTREME MACHINES

THE WORLD'S DIRTIEST MACHINES

Jennifer Blizin Gillis

Raintree

Chicago, Illinois

www.heinemannraintree.com
Visit our website to find out more information about Heinemann-Raintree books.

To order:
☎ Phone 888-454-2279
💻 Visit www.heinemannraintree.com to browse our catalog and order online.

© 2011 Raintree
an imprint of Capstone Global Library, LLC
Chicago, Illinois

Edited by Nancy Dickmann and Megan Cotugno
Designed by Jo Hinton-Malivoire
Picture research by Tracy Cummins
Production by Victoria Fitzgerald

Printed and bound in China by CTPS

14 13 12 11 10
10 9 8 7 6 5 4 3 2 1

Library of Congress Cataloging-in-Publication Data
Gillis, Jennifer Blizin, 1950-
  The world's dirtiest machines / Jennifer Blizin Gillis.
    p. cm. -- (Extreme machines)
  Includes bibliographical references and index.
  ISBN 978-1-4109-3876-3 (hc) -- ISBN 978-1-4109-3882-4 (pb) 1. Machinery--Juvenile literature. I. Title.
  TJ147.G54 2011
  628--dc22
                            2009051228

Acknowledgments
The author and publishers are grateful to the following for permission to reproduce copyright material: Alamy p. **21** (Peter Titmuss); Corbis pp. **10** (© Gerd Ludwig), **12** (© Steve Crisp/Reuters), **13** (© Koen van Weel /Reuters), **14** (© Joel W. Rogers), **15** (© Alan Schein Photography), **17** (© Ashley Cooper), **24** (© Al Satterwhite/Transtock), **27** (© Richard Hamilton Smith); Getty Images pp. **4** (WIN-Initiative), **18** (Paul Chesley), **20** (Ken Welsh), **25** (AFP/FAYEZ NURELDINE); istockphoto p. **7** (© Mike Clarke); Photolibrary pp. **6** (Andreas Schlegel), **11** (Imagesource Imagesource); Shutterstock pp. **5** (© Nethunter), **8** (© SergioZ), **9** (© SergioZ), **16** (© Sergios), **19** (© Zacarias Pereira da Mata), **22** (© Liz Van Steenburgh), **23** (© tomazzi), **26** (© Dmitry Naumov).

Cover photograph of full track loader reproduced with permission of Corbis (© Jim Zuckerman).

Every effort has been made to contact copyright holders of any material reproduced in this book. Any omissions will be rectified in subsequent printings if notice is given to the publisher.

Some words are shown in bold, **like this**. You can find out what they mean by looking in the glossary.

Contents

Doing Dirty Work

All over the world, there are dirty jobs to do. Dirty machines help with this dirty work. Dirty machines dig, suck, smash, and dump.

⬇ The world can be a dirty place. Dirty machines help keep it clean.

5

Garbage Getters

Garbage trucks pick up solid waste. Some have **hydraulic** arms that pick up garbage cans. Workers throw garbage into the **hopper** on other trucks. A huge blade slashes and smashes the trash so the hopper can hold more.

hydraulic arm

hopper

EXTREME FACT
A full truck holds up to 14 tons of trash. That is a lot of garbage!

Trash Smashers

Garbage trucks dump their loads in **landfills.** Landfill **compactors** roll over the mountains of trash. They have spiked metal wheels. Their blades push and smash the trash to make room for more.

blade

spikes

EXTREME FACT

The Caterpillar 836H landfill compactor weighs almost 120,000 pounds. That's as much as six school buses!

Dirty Tractors

Tractors on a farm need to get dirty. Some have **mulchers** attached that break up the dirt. This makes it easier to plant seeds.

Tractors do other jobs too. When the land is ready, they plant the seeds. Then they water them. These can be dirty jobs!

Filthy Ships

Dredgers are boats that pull up sand, dirt, and rocks from underwater. Long hoses reach deep down. They suck up the sand at the bottom of rivers and oceans. Some dredgers pump sand out onto shore.

A hose under this ship is sucking up sand.

EXTREME FACT

The largest dredgers have hoppers that can hold enough sand to fill more than 10,000 sandboxes!

Barges are open ships shaped like rectangles. They carry trash and dirty loads. Some garbage trucks dump their loads into barges. The barges float the garbage to **landfills.**

coal

scrap metal

↑ Nets keep the
garbage from
blowing into
the water.

15

Dirty Excavators

Excavators are powerful shovels. They have a long arm called a boom. A bucket on the end scoops up heavy loads. Excavators can pick up trees or knock down buildings. An attachment called a thumb pinches and pulls.

boom

bucket

thumb

17

Dump Trucks

Dump trucks carry away dirt and other trash. Other machines fill the dump truck. The loads can weigh hundreds of tons. Dump trucks have more than two wheels in the back to carry these heavy loads.

double wheels

dump box

A **hydraulic system** uses oil to push up one end of the dump box. This tips the box, so that the load slides out the back.

Off-Road Dumpers

In mines and **quarries,** dump trucks go up and down steep hills. The cab and truck bed of **articulated dump trucks** move separately. This keeps the truck from tipping over.

bed

cab

This truck is moving sand to make room for a new road in a tunnel.

21

Dirty 'Dozers

What can clean up tons of mud? Bulldozers! Some bulldozers have giant tires that help them drive through sand or mud. Bulldozers use different blades to push their heavy loads. A u-blade is the most common. It is curved.

u-blade

tracks

Most of these big machines move on tracks.

Fun and Dirty

Huge engines roar. At a mud drag race, cars and trucks fly down a short, flat, muddy track. As the race cars take off, mud sprays everywhere.

There are many kinds of mud racing vehicles. People make changes to their cars, trucks, and SUVs so they can go faster in mud races.

All-terrain vehicles (ATVs) race in mud, too. In Championship Mud Racing, riders run their ATVs around an oval track where mud can be up to four feet deep!

EXTREME FACT

The dirtiest machines of all may be ATV mud boggers. Their extra large tires keep them rolling through mud pits. Long tubes called snorkels let air into their engines but keep mud out.

Test Yourself!

Match each sentence with the correct vehicle.

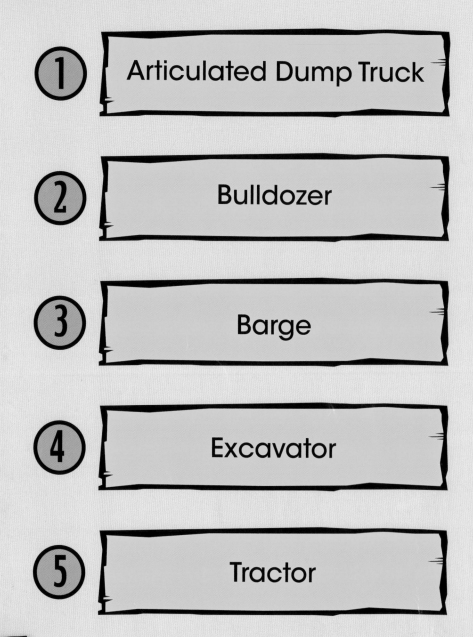

1. Articulated Dump Truck

2. Bulldozer

3. Barge

4. Excavator

5. Tractor

a This dirty machine breaks up dirt on a farm.

b The long arm on this dirty machine is called a boom.

c This kind of dirty truck can climb steep hills in mines or quarries.

d These dirty machines have blades that can scrape up mud.

e Flat-bottomed boats like these carry dirty loads.

Glossary

articulated dump truck vehicle built with sections that can move by themselves

compactor machine that can crush things to save space

dredger machine that takes sand, dirt, and rocks from underwater

excavator large machine used for digging and pulling

hopper container that can hold large amounts

hydraulic moved by the power of liquid, such as water or oil, being forced through a narrow tube

landfill large piece of land where garbage is buried in between layers of dirt

mulcher machine that breaks up dirt on farms

quarry open pit where rock or stone is dug out by machine

Find Out More

Books

Alinas, Marv. *Bulldozers.* Mankato, MN: Child's World, 2008.

Gilbert, Sara. *Dump Trucks.* Mankato, MN: The Creative Company, 2009.

Poolos, Jamie. *Wild About ATVs.* NY: Powerkids Press, 2008.

Spalding, Lee-Anne. *Off-road Racing.* Vero Beach, FL: Rourke, 2009.

Websites

Caterpillar Trucks
http://www.cat.com/equipment
Pictures and descriptions of all of the heavy equipment made by Caterpillar, including trash compactors, dump trucks, excavators, and more.

Mud Racers
http://www.mudracersassociation.com
Information about all kinds of muddy off-road races and vehicles, plus detailed action photos.

More Extreme Machines
http://www.worsleyschool.net/science/files/extreme/machines.html
Pictures and descriptions of some of the biggest construction vehicles on Earth.

Find out

What is a Knuckleboom Loader?

Index